# LOOK IT UP
Now in a fully revised edition

**Photo Credits**: Austin Rover Group Ltd; Chris Barker; Bedford Commercial Vehicles Ltd; BIP Chemicals Ltd; Paul Brierly; Camera Press; J. Allan Cash; Central Electricity Generating Board; Citroën; Coles Cranes; Doxford Engines; Dunlop-Angus; ESAB Automation Ltd; Mary Evans; Massey Ferguson; Peter Gardner; Michael Holford; Imperial Business Equipment Ltd; Ingersol-Rand Co.; Robin Kerrod; Dick Makin; S.Martin; Mercedes-Benz; Herbert Morris; Quadrant Picture Library; G.R.Roberts; Rolls Royce; Seiko; Sony (U.K.) Ltd.; Theorem; Trend Communications Ltd; Vickers PLC; John Watney; Thomas A. Wilkie Co. Ltd.; Woolf Tools; ZEFA.

**Front cover**: Ferranti Scottish Group.

**Illustrations**: Jim Bamber; Dick Eastland; Philip Emms; Dan Escott; Elizabeth Graham-Yool; Colin Hawkins; Eric Jewell; Giles Hollingworth; Ben Manchipp; Stephanie Manchipp; David Palmer; Mike Roffe; Barry Salter; Roger Walker; Michael Whelply.

First edition © Macmillan Publishers Limited, 1980
Reprinted in 1981, 1982, 1983 and 1984
Second edition © Macmillan Publishers Limited, 1985
Reprinted in 1986, 1987, 1988

## Chief Educational Adviser
Lynda Snowdon

## Teacher Advisory Panel
Helen Craddock, John Enticknap, Arthur Razzell

## Editorial Board
Jan Burgess, Rosemary Canter, Philip M. Clark, Beatrice Phillpotts, Sue Seddon, Philip Steele

## Picture Researchers
Caroline Adams, Anne Marie Ehrlich, Gayle Hayter, Ethel Hurwicz, Pat Hodgson, Stella Martin, Frances Middlestorb

## Designer
Keith Faulkner

## Contributors and consultants
John E. Allen, Neil Ardley, Sue Becklake, Robert Burton, Barry Cox, Jacqueline Dineen, David J. Fletcher, Plantagenet Somerset Fry, Bill Gunston, Robin Kerrod, Mark Lambert, Anne Millard, Kaye Orten, Ian Ridpath, Peter Stephens, Nigel Swann, Aubrey Tulley, Tom Williamson, Thomas Wright

Published by Macmillan Children's Books a division of Macmillan Publishers Limited 4 Little Essex Street, London WC2R 3LF Associated companies throughout the world

ISBN 0-333-39730-4 (volume 12)
ISBN 0-333-39568-9 (complete set)

Printed in Hong Kong

# The World of Machines

Second Edition

LOOK IT UP

# Contents

# MACHINES ALL AROUND

Long ago there were no machines.
Everything had to be done by hand.
Today there are many machines.
They help us in many ways. We use
them at home, on farms, and in
factories. There are machines for use
on land, on the sea, and in the air.
Some have many parts. Other
machines have very few.

clock

axe

concrete mixer

shovel

wheelbarrow

4

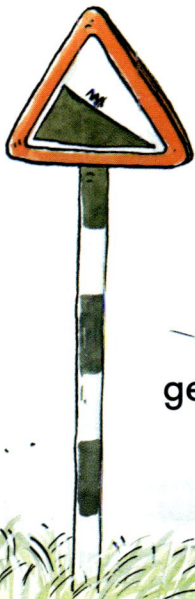

brake

brake

gears

pedal

slope

tyres

ad drill

wheels

brake

# Wheels and gears

The wheel is a simple machine. It is also an important part of more complicated machines. The wheel was invented about 7000 years ago. Men wanted to carry heavy loads. They put wheels onto carts. The wheels went round easily on rough ground. Later wheeled carts called chariots were used in war.

wheel    axle

fairground big wheel

Life today would be very different without wheels. There would be no cars, clocks, clockwork toys, or rides at the fairground. Wheels are important for engines, drills, and other kinds of turning machines.

Wheels are useful for the models you make. You can use them to make things roll along. Have you ever used them to make pulleys or to lift things?

You can use round boxes and corrugated paper to make gearwheels. The slots on the edges fit into each other. The gearwheels turn in opposite ways.

Before the wheel was invented men dragged things along the ground. Then they found it was easier to move things on rollers. Later they cut thin slices off rollers. These made wheels.

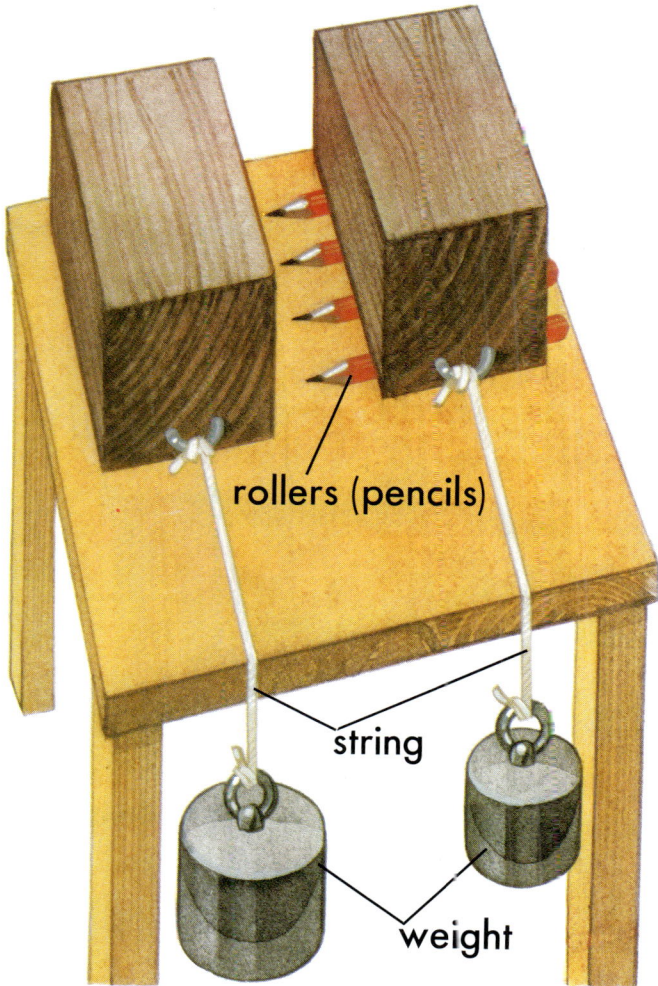

spiral thread

winding handle

string

weight

The roller above has a winding handle. The roller is turned to wind up the rope and bucket. This is called a wheel and axle.

rollers (pencils)

string

weight

Find out if it is easier to roll something or to drag it along. You need two identical objects. Put rollers under one of them. Which one do you think will move more easily? Which needs a stronger pull?

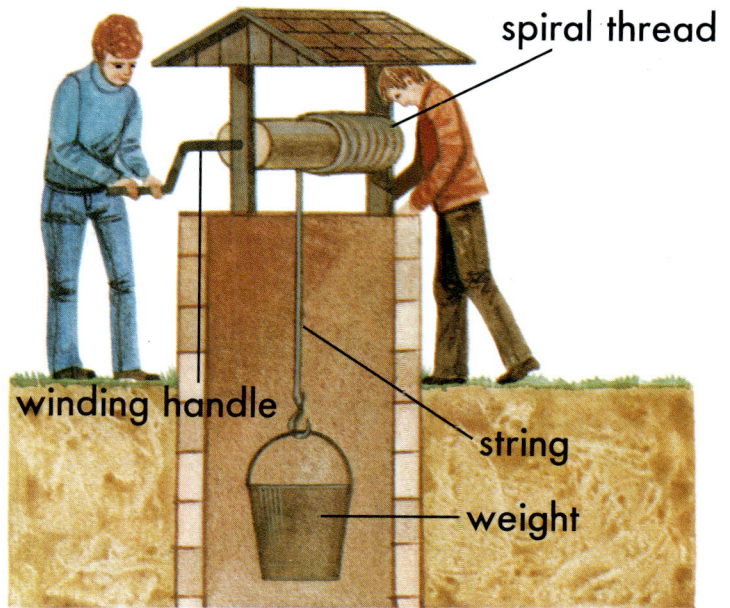

pulley

The pulley is another kind of wheel. It has a groove all the way round the edge. The rope fits into this groove. It is much easier to pull a heavy load in this way.

## Levers

The lever is the simplest machine we use. A bar is a very simple lever when it is on a support. It moves or pivots on the thing supporting it.

A spade is also a lever. The blade pivots on the earth. The handle is longer than the blade. This gives the man digging power to lever the soil.

A pair of nutcrackers is a lever. The long handles give us more power to crack the nut.

Look at the see-saw in the picture above. The see-saw is a lever. It is supported in the middle. The plank pivots on the stand.

A burglar uses a jemmy. It is used like a spade to lever things open. The long handle gives extra leverage.

# Wedges and screws

A wedge is another very simple machine. Its shape is very important. If you lay a wedge flat on the ground you can see it slopes. A ramp is a wedge. People in wheelchairs find the slope of a ramp very useful. Stairs are a kind of wedge too. They make it easier for us to climb upwards.

wedge

A wedge can be used to split logs. The thin end is hammered further and further down into the wood. The slope pushes the sides of the log apart and the log splits open. After a while the log splits in two.

Have you ever come down a helter skelter? It is a slope that goes round in the shape of a spiral.

screw thread

The spirals of a screw look like a helter skelter. These spirals are called the thread.

# In the home

Today we have many machines to help us in the home. In the kitchen we use machines for peeling, chopping and grinding food. We use mixers to mix ingredients together for cooking. Refrigerators and deep-freezers help to keep the food fresh. How many other machines can you see here?

cooker hood

pressure cooker

hot plate

washing machine

dishwasher

whisk

mixer-blender

sieve

fridge-freezer

refrigerator section

hedge-cutter

hover mower

battery clock

coffee maker

freezer section

mincer

vacuum cleaner

can opener

kitchen scales

lemon squeezer

hand grinder

steam iron

toaster

grater

electric kettle

pestle and mortar

11

# Home helpers

Household chores can be very hard work and can take a lot of time. People have invented all kinds of machines to make life easier for us. For hundreds of years, clothes had to be washed by hand, and floors had to be scrubbed every day. Today we use electric washing machines, and we clean floors with electric polishers and vacuum cleaners. Here are some of the most useful household machines.

Beating the dust out of carpets by hand is a messy job. These days we use a vacuum cleaner instead. A roller loosens the dust in the carpet. An electric fan sucks up the dust into a bag. When the bag is full you can empty it in the dustbin.

People used to spend hours preparing food so that it would last a long time. Today we use refrigerators and freezers to keep food fresh.

This is a front-loading automatic washing machine. Inside is a drum which turns round and round. The clothes are washed clean as they are tumbled round and round in soapy water.

## Tools and gadgets

We use many different tools and gadgets in the home. They are all machines even if they look simple. Each of them is made up of different parts. Levers, wedges, screws and wheels are often used in these machines. Here are a few of the machines we use. They help us in all sorts of ways.

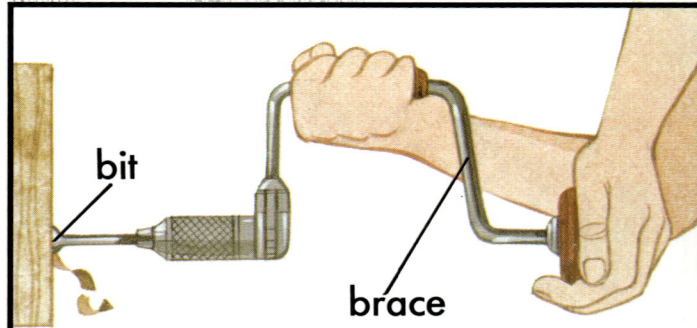

bit

brace

This brace and bit drills holes in wood. The brace turns the bit.

This wall can opener grips and turns the can with two wheels.

The drill in this picture uses gears to turn the bit round.

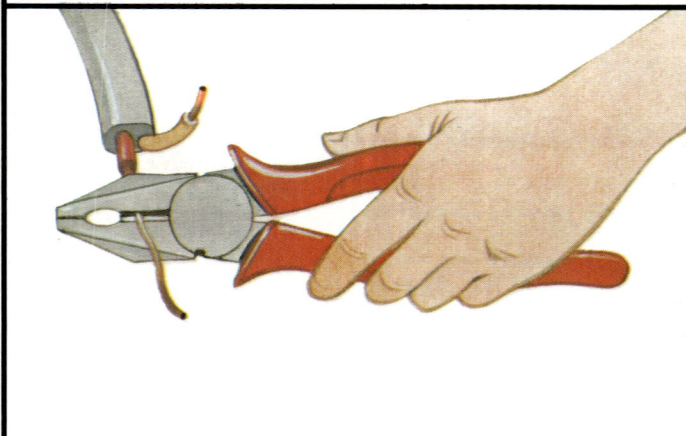

Pliers are used for gripping and cutting wire.

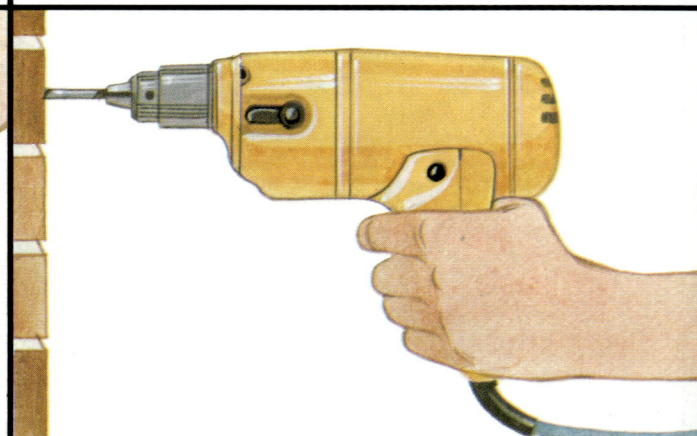

An electric drill uses an electric motor to turn the bit.

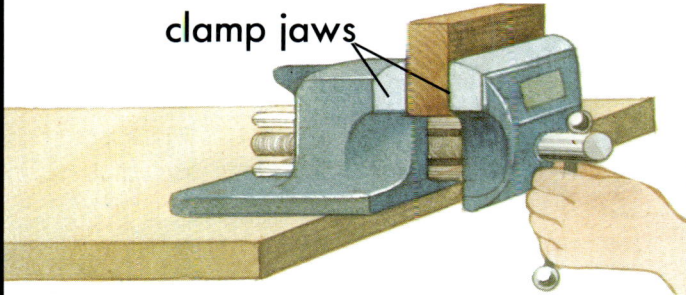

The vice is opened and closed by turning the screw with the lever.

Here we are using the screwdriver as a lever to open the lid.

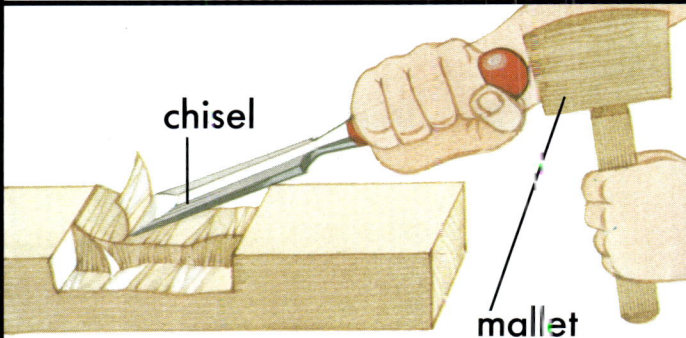

The cutting edge of a chisel is like a wedge. It splits the wood.

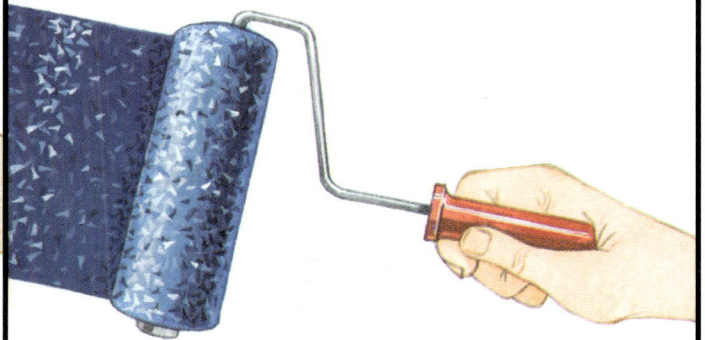

A roller can be used to paint a wall instead of a brush.

This wrench has lever handles. They make the ends grip tightly.

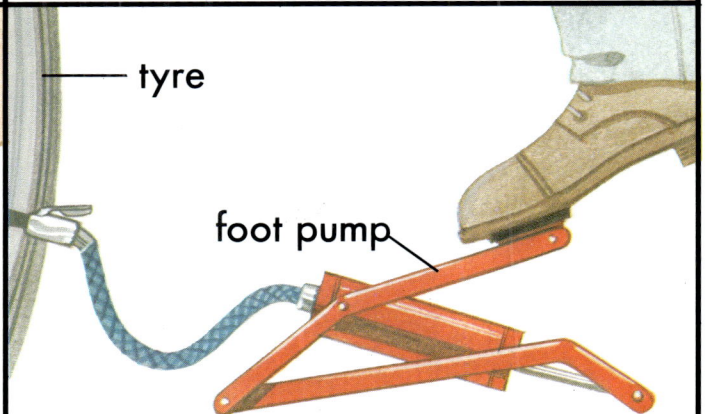

The lever on a foot pump is used to force air into tyres.

# Clocks and clockwork

Until a few years ago all clocks were made with little gearwheels, which turned the hands. Most of them were powered by a spring. We call this clockwork. The old lantern clocks shown below worked in this way.

Many modern clocks work in a different way. The one on the right is an electronic clock. It shows the time in numbers, or digits. This clock also has a radio attached.

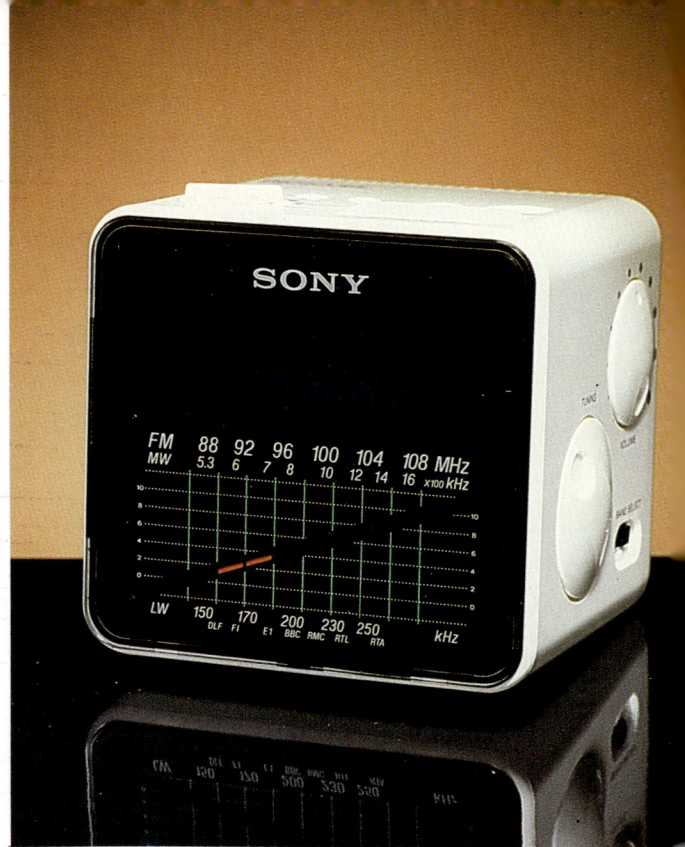

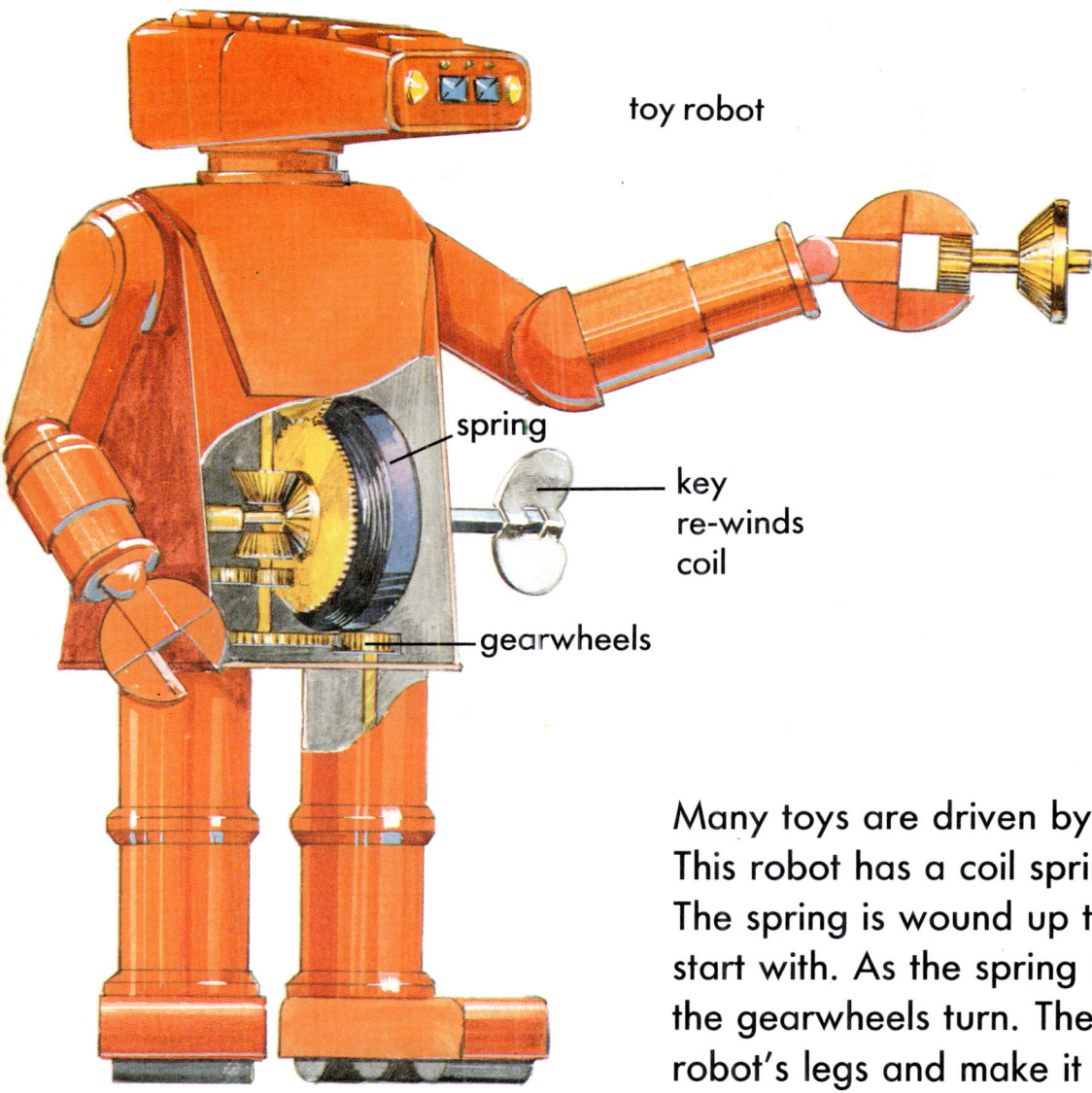

toy robot

spring

key
re-winds
coil

gearwheels

Many toys are driven by clockwork.
This robot has a coil spring inside.
The spring is wound up tightly to
start with. As the spring unwinds
the gearwheels turn. They move the
robot's legs and make it walk.

This is the inside of a musical box.
It works by clockwork. The handle is
turned. This turns a gear. The gear
turns the gearwheel and the cylinder.
You can see tiny pins on the cylinder
in the picture. These tiny pins hit
pieces of metal in a special order.
The sound of the pins hitting the
metal makes a tune.

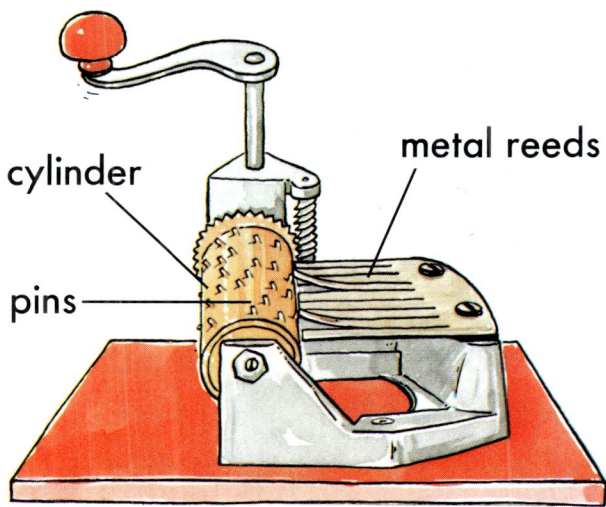

cylinder

metal reeds

pins

## In the garden

There is always a lot of work to be done in the garden. Lawns need to be cut. Hedges have to be trimmed. Bushes need to be cut back to encourage new growth. The gardener uses machines to help him. Many are simple machines with few parts. The lawnmower is a more complicated machine.

An electric hedge trimmer has two cutting blades with sharp teeth. They look like the blades of a saw. One stays still. The other moves quickly backwards and forwards.

The electric lawnmower above has a sharp blade which lies flat on the grass. It cuts as it goes round. The cable carries electricity from the house to work the motor. It makes cutting the grass much easier.

pruning shears

The lawnmower shown below is called a hover mower. It cuts the grass while it hovers a few centimetres above the ground. It lifts itself above the ground on a 'cushion' of air. The cutter is a sharp blade that spins round fast.

milking parlour

milk container

## ON THE FARM

Years ago there were more farmers than there are today. Now fewer farmers produce more food than ever before. They have machines to help them. Machines help to prepare the ground for planting. They help to harvest the crops. The most useful farm machines are the tractor and the combine harvester.

grain silo

tractor

hay turner

grass cutter

# Farm machines

Years ago horses pulled all the machines used on the farm. Today tractors do their work. Unlike horses, tractors can be driven all day without getting tired.
Farmers use tractors to pull all kinds of machines, such as ploughs, drills and sprayers.

In the picture on the right, you see a tractor pulling a plough. The blades of the plough dig deeply into the soil. They turn it over and bury the weeds on top of the ground.

In the picture below, the tractor is pulling a seed drill. This machine sows seeds under the surface.

The tractor above is carrying spray equipment. This is used to spray the growing crops with chemicals. These chemicals help kill pests which might harm the crops and cause disease.

Tractors are powerful machines. Some have a diesel engine. Others have a petrol engine. Most tractors have huge wheels at the back. These give them pulling power. Some tractors have 'caterpillar' tracks. They are used on heavy, wet ground.

23

# Harvesters

Month after month, the farmer looks after his crops. He may spray them with weedkillers to prevent the weeds growing among them. He may scatter fertilisers over them to make them grow better. Then at last the crops are ripe, and it is time for the harvest. Today almost all farm crops are harvested by machines. The most important machine is the combine harvester. It is mainly used to harvest grain crops such as wheat.

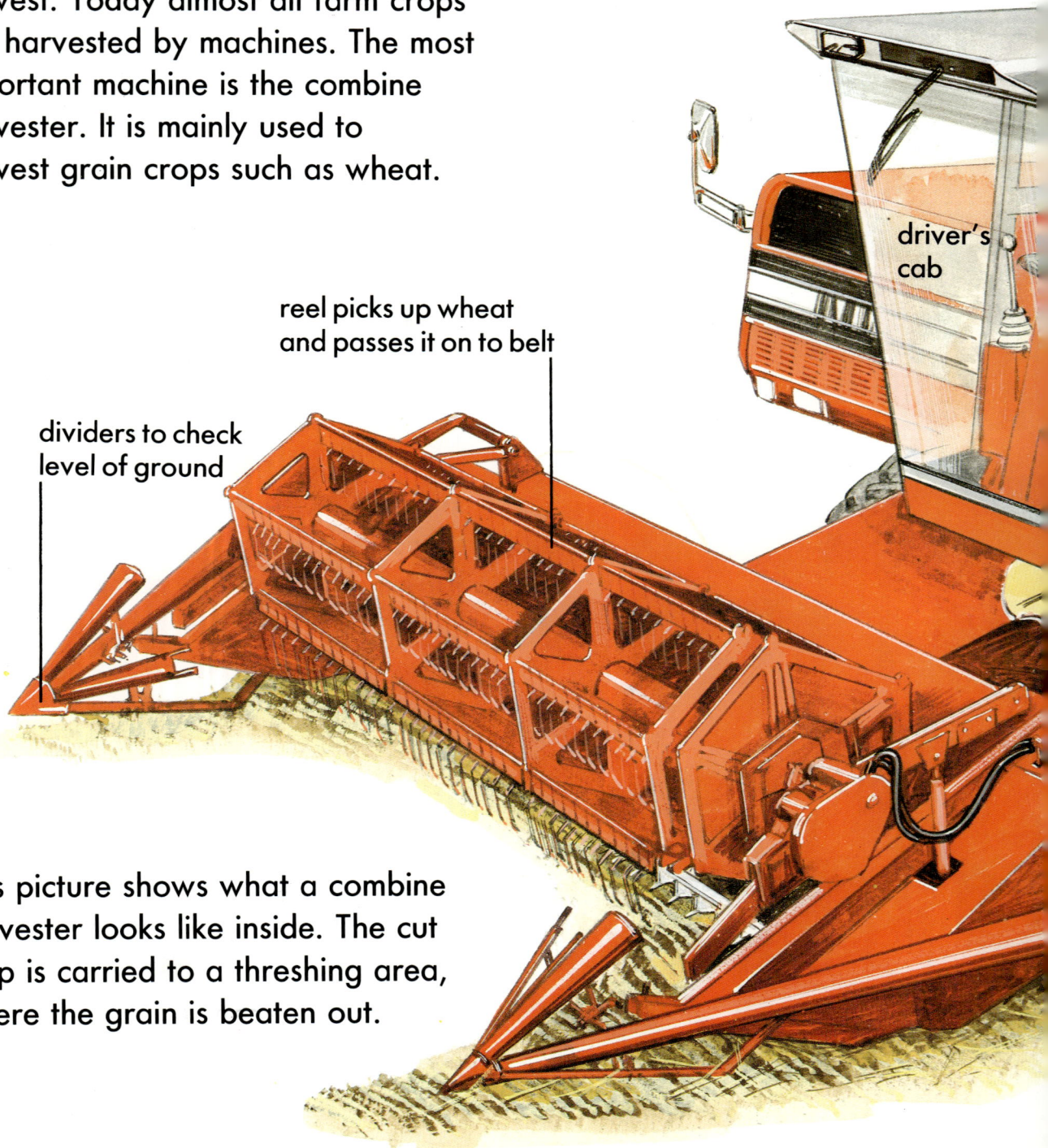

reel picks up wheat and passes it on to belt

driver's cab

dividers to check level of ground

This picture shows what a combine harvester looks like inside. The cut crop is carried to a threshing area, where the grain is beaten out.

Many different machines have been
made to harvest different crops.
The machine on the left is harvesting
sugar beet. This is a root crop used
to make sugar. The machine on the
right is harvesting maize.

unloading arm
for grain

straw
spreader

grain carried
upwards

beater

sieves

beater

The combine harvester does two jobs.
First it reaps, or cuts the crop. Then it
threshes the crop, or separates
the grain from the stalks.

# IN THE TOWN

Often old buildings are pulled down. Then new ones are put up. Heavy machines help in many ways. They clear the ground. They dig the foundations. They put up frames for the new buildings. Machines are useful too in busy office blocks. How many machines can you see in this picture?

tower crane

hole borer

mixer truck

girders

concrete foundations

dump truck

26

bulldozer

truck crane

:avator

# Cranes and excavators

Cranes are used for lifting things. They have a long arm, which can swing in all directions. It carries a long cable with a hook at the end. This is hooked to the object to be lifted. The crane on the right is called a tower crane. You can see it on building sites carrying steel girders and buckets of cement.

The crane shown above is called a truck crane. It has its own engine and is driven about like an ordinary truck. When it is working, it puts down four 'feet', and the wheels lift off the ground. With its 'feet' down, it can lift heavy loads without tipping over.

You can also see different kinds of digging machines on building sites. They are called excavators. The excavator on the left has digging buckets at the front and back. Here the driver is using a bucket to knock down a wall.

The picture above shows a grab excavator. The scoop is dropped into the mud. Its jaws clamp together and then the scoop is raised.

# People movers

An American, Elisha Otis, invented the first lift over 100 years ago. Before that there were no very tall buildings. People did not want to climb too many stairs. Lifts only carry a few people at a time and are expensive to build. A moving staircase or escalator can carry more people more quickly.

The picture above shows another kind of people mover. People travel on a moving rubber belt. You often see these 'moving walkways' at airports.

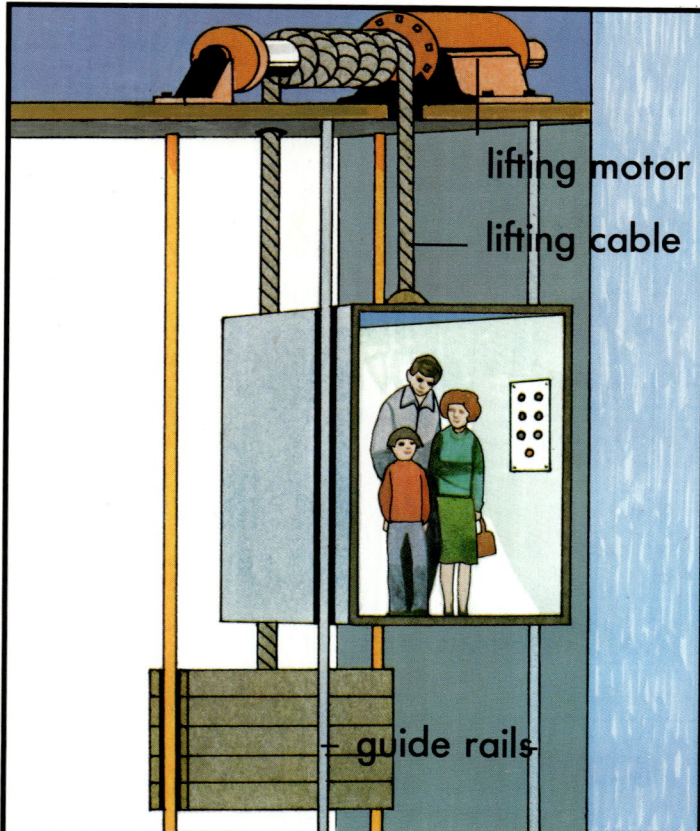

lifting motor

lifting cable

guide rails

A cable pulls the lift up and lets it down. An electric motor controls the winding cable. The lift slides up and down between guide rails.

steps begin to rise

steps folded flat

toothed wheel

winding cable

endless chain

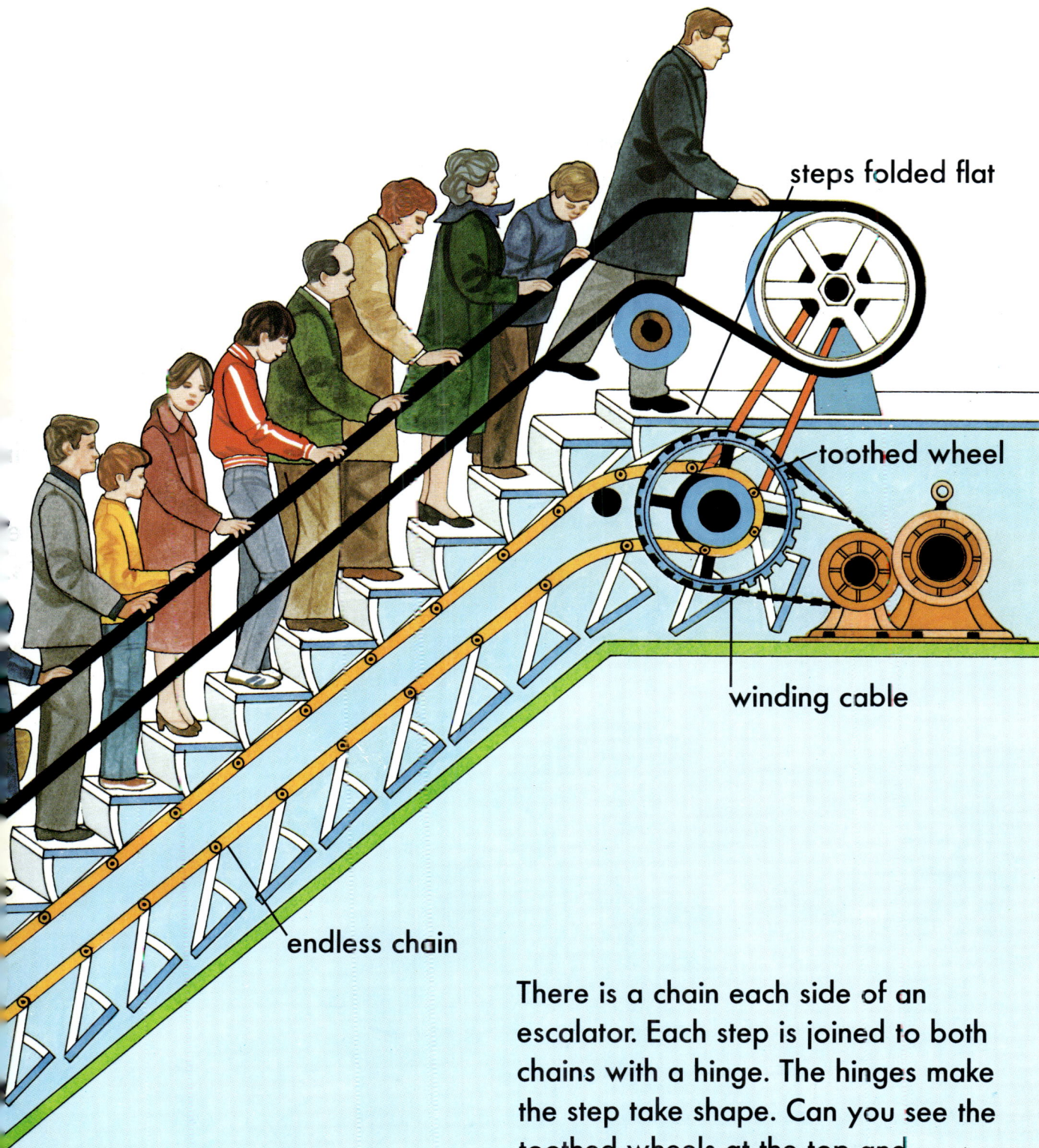

There is a chain each side of an escalator. Each step is joined to both chains with a hinge. The hinges make the step take shape. Can you see the toothed wheels at the top and bottom of the chains? An electric motor turns one of these wheels. The chains and steps then move round.

# Office machines

Office workers now have many machines to speed up their work. They use typewriters to write letters quickly and neatly. They copy letters and other documents with a photocopier. They send typed messages around the world with a Telex machine. Many offices also use a computer to work things out.

The picture above shows some early typewriters.

The Telex machine below changes typed messages into electrical signal These pass along telephone wires. A the other end of the wires another Telex types out the message.

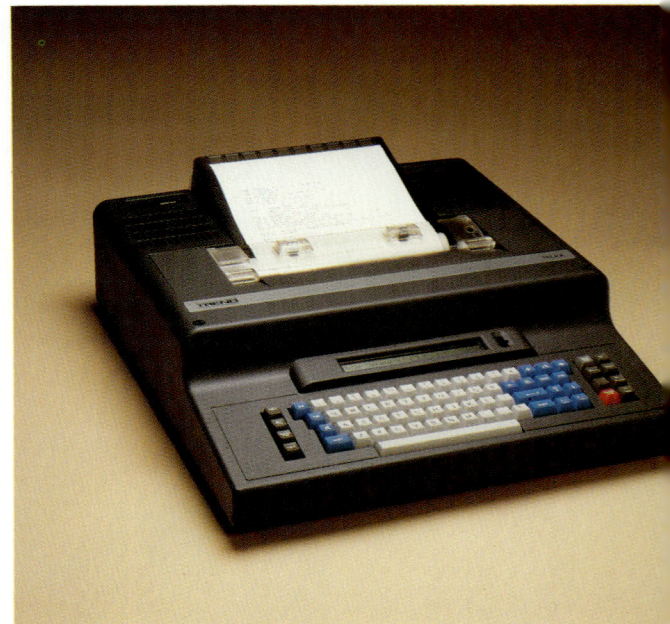

The picture shows one of the latest kinds of typewriter. It is called an electronic typewriter. You type on the keyboard, and the words appear on a separate printer.

SE 1020

ADLER

TA

33

# Computers at work

The computer is an electronic machine. It works by tiny pulses of electricity. Computers were first used just to make calculations. Now they have thousands of uses. In factories they run machines. In space they guide spacecraft. Home computers can be used for playing games – or for homework!

The most important part of a computer is a tiny crystal slice. It is called a microchip. You can see one on the left. The microchips act as the 'brains' of a computer.

Information for computers can be stored in many ways. The picture on the right shows four methods

The computer in the picture below is working a special X-ray machine. This is 'scanning' or looking inside the head of the patient.

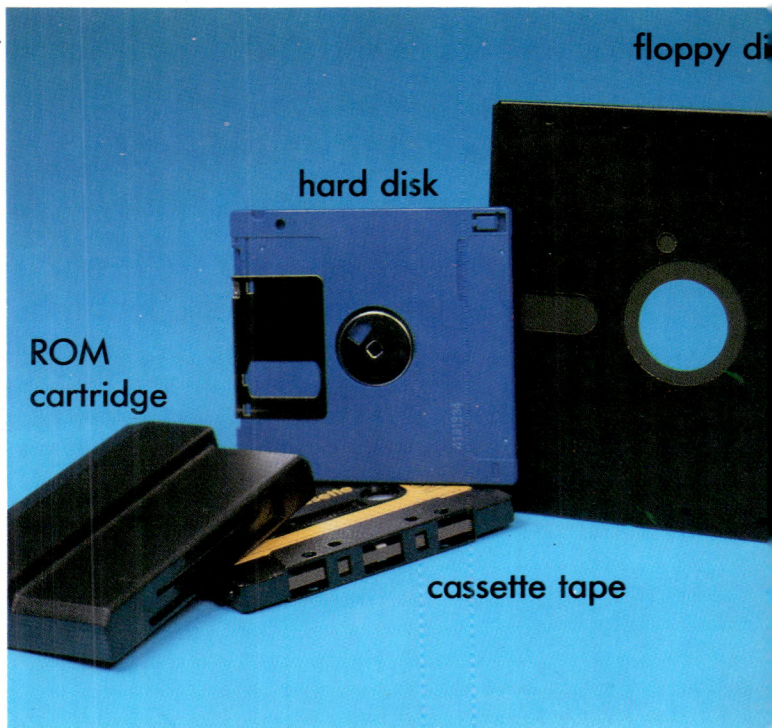

floppy disk

hard disk

ROM cartridge

cassette tape

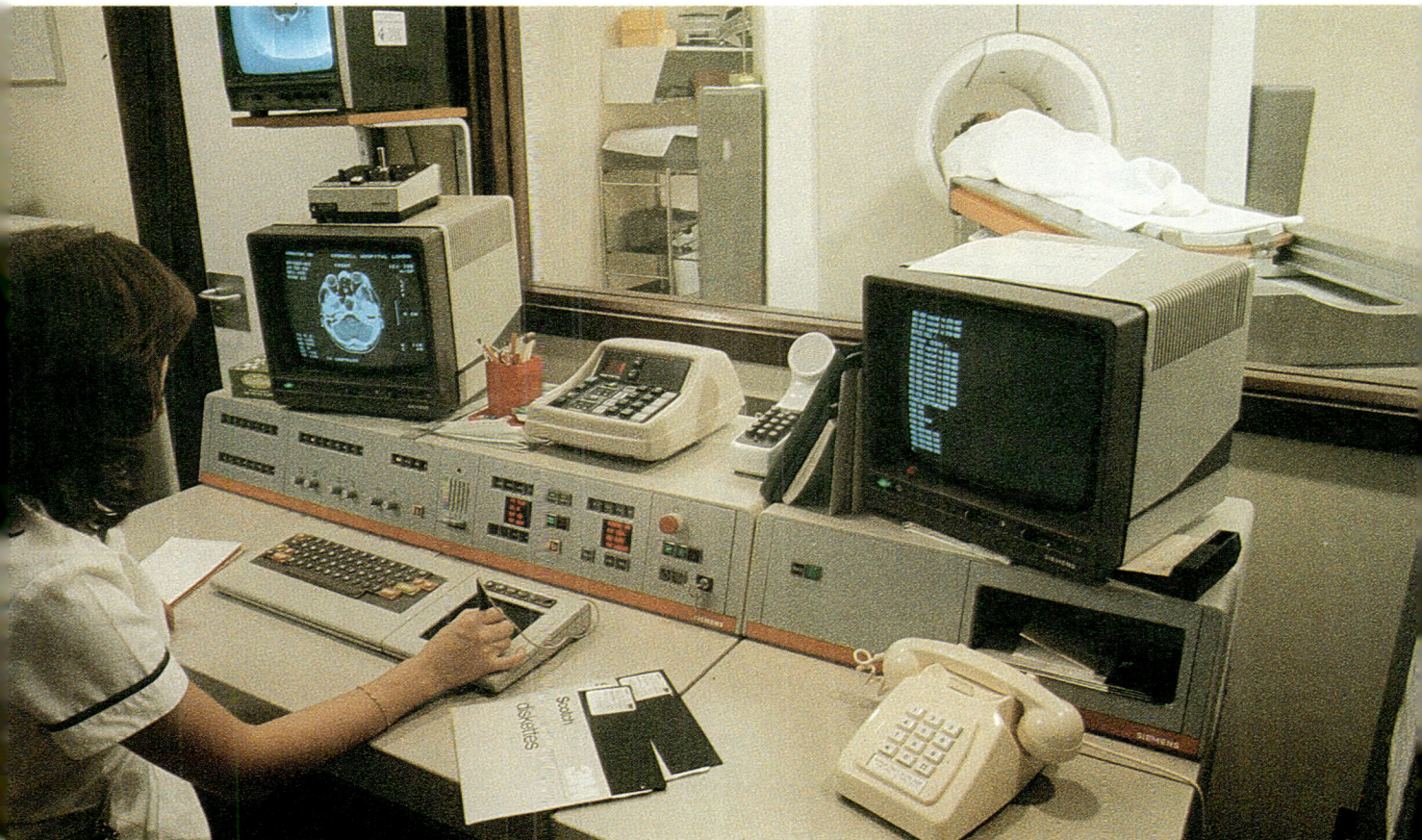

# IN THE FACTORY

Many years ago factories were small. The workers used their hands to make and repair things. This way of working was very slow. Modern factories are large. They employ many workers, who use all kinds of machines to speed up their work. The workers on the right are using electric sewing machines to make chair covers.

The picture above shows another factory. The workers are seated along a moving belt. This is called a 'production line' or 'assembly line'. Different parts of machinery are passed down the line, and fitted together by the workers. Factories which make goods in this way can produce goods in very large numbers at high speed.

Most cars are made on a production line like the one below. The cars move slowly through the factory on a conveyor belt, which is a bit like a miniature railway. The workers stand beside the conveyor and work on each car as it passes by. They carry out the same work on each car and learn how to do it quickly.

Other work is done by machines.

# Factory tools

Many factories make things out of metal. The metal has to be cut to shape, and is often drilled and polished. Because metal is so hard and tough, the cutting, drilling and polishing must be done by power tools. They are called machine tools. They are driven by powerful electric motors.

Metal is prepared for cutting by a special machine tool known as a profile cutter.

Many factories produce plastic goods. Plastic is normally shaped by squeezing and moulding.

The picture shows a machine tool called a lathe. It turns the large shaft round. A sharp tool presses against the shaft and cuts it to shape.

# Robots

In some modern factories machines do work human workers once carried out. They have 'arms' and 'hands' to hold tools and pick up things, and they can move these parts like we can. These machines are kinds of robots. Factory robots do not look like human beings. Some robots have been made that do look like humans. We call them androids. One day androids may help us in the home. We could teach them to do the cleaning or cook.

The robot arm above has a light touch. It can pick up a piece of ice without crushing it. In factories like the one on the right, robots are often used to weld metal parts together. It is safer than using humans.

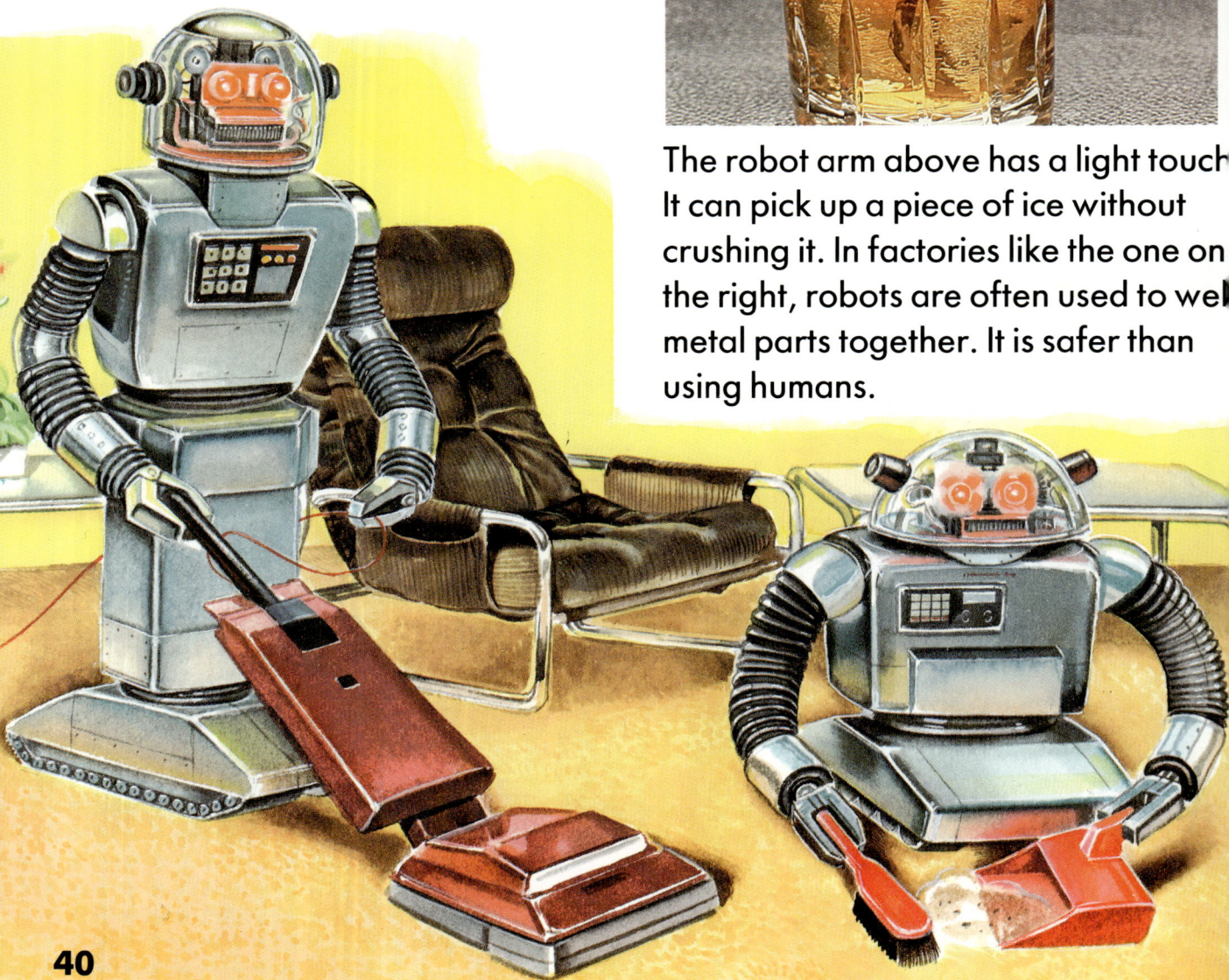

## ON THE ROAD

Cars and motorcycles are very complicated machines. The first cars were built about 100 years ago. They looked like horse carriages, but they had engines. Today engines are more powerful. People take their cars to filling stations like this one to get petrol. Mechanics mend cars.

# Bicycles

Riding on a bicycle, or 'bike', is good fun. It is also a cheap way to travel because you use no fuel. On a racing bike like the one below you can travel as fast as 30 kilometres per hour. It has ten gears. Using the gears you can pedal more easily up hills and go faster over level ground.

The picture on the right shows a rider on a BMX bike. The bike is built especially strong so that the rider can do acrobatics on it.

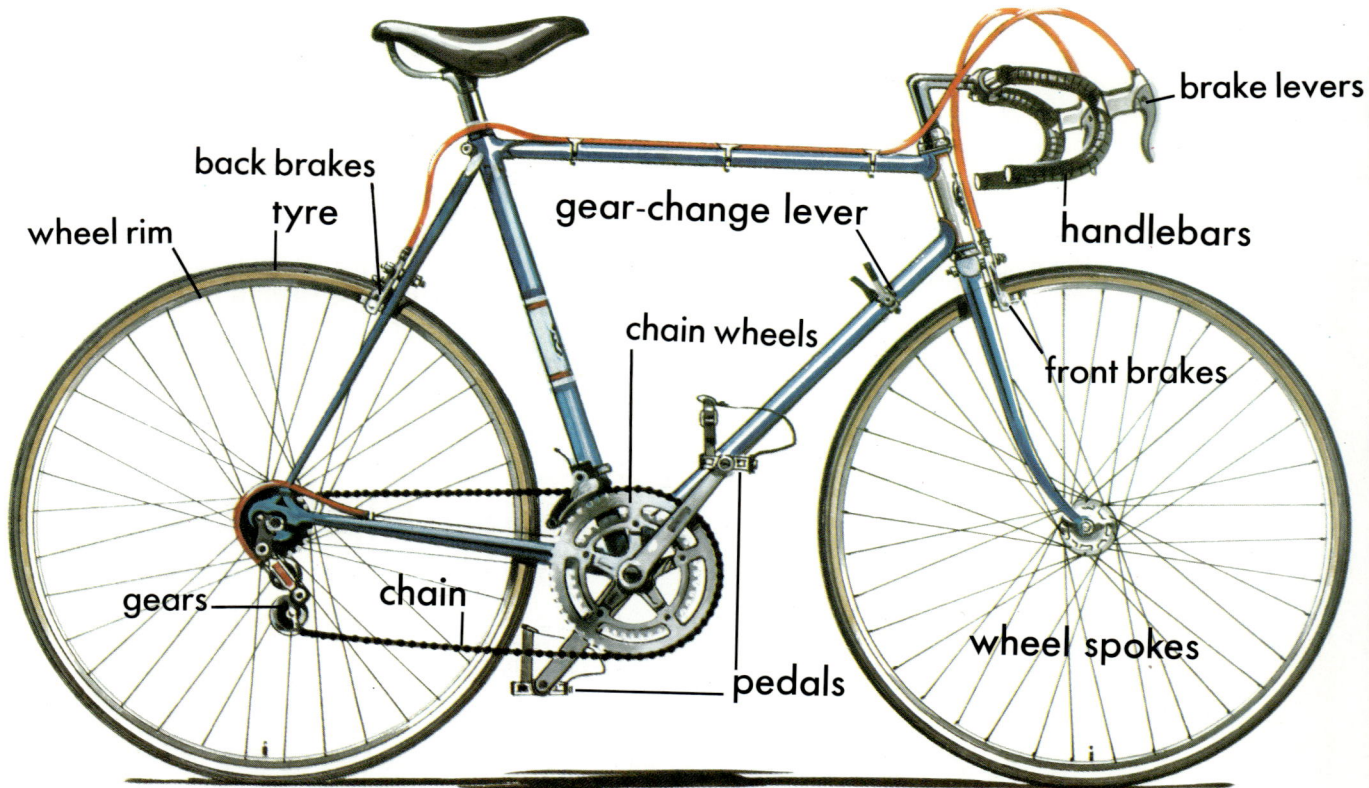

brake levers

back brakes

tyre

wheel rim

gear-change lever

handlebars

chain wheels

front brakes

gears

chain

wheel spokes

pedals

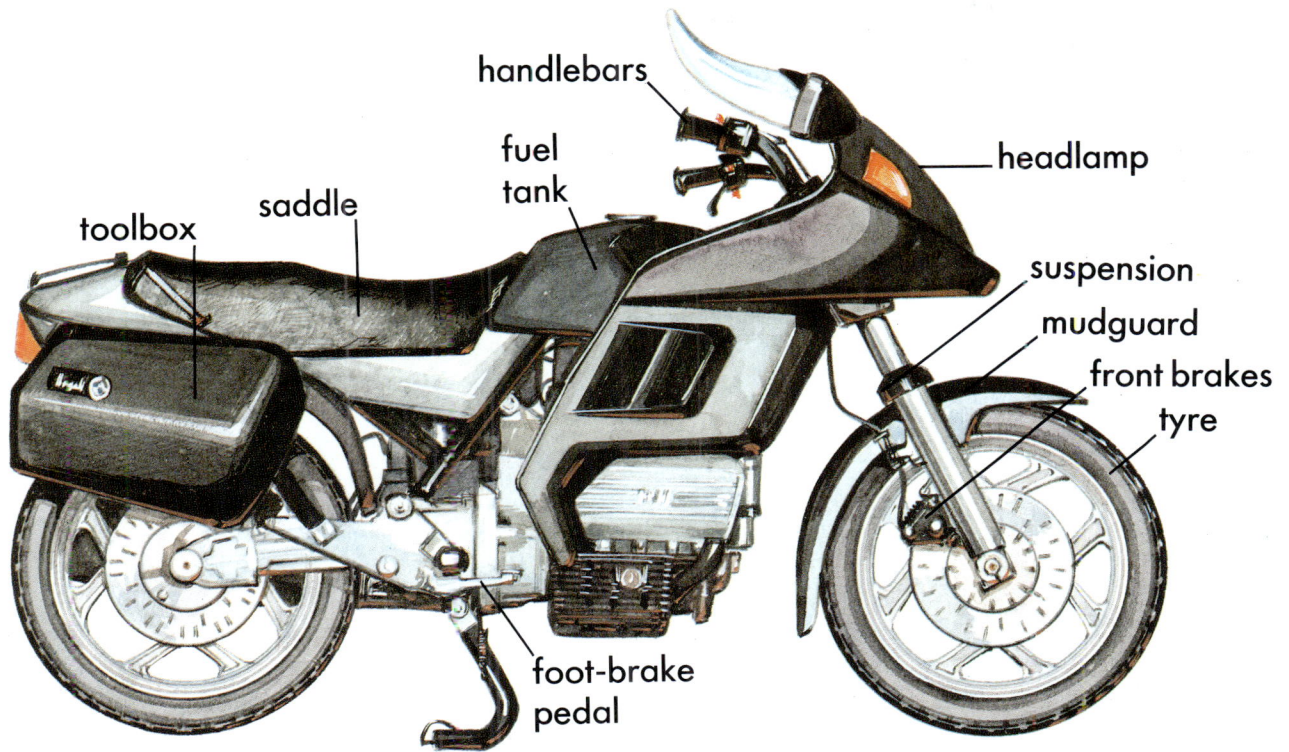

handlebars

fuel
tank

headlamp

toolbox

saddle

suspension

mudguard

front brakes

tyre

foot-brake
pedal

## Motorcycles

Motorcycles, or 'motorbikes', have a petrol engine. In most motorbikes the engine drives a chain that turns the back wheels. In others, the back wheels are turned by a shaft. On most motorbikes, the engine is started by stamping on the kick-starter. On some it is started by pressing a self-starter, which works by electricity. Many motorbikes can travel at speeds of up to 150 kilometres per hour. Police motorbikes like the one on the left can travel much faster.

## Motor vehicles

Vehicles of one kind or another have been used for over 5,000 years. At first they were pulled by oxen and horses. But about 100 years ago a new type of vehicle was invented. People called it a 'horseless carriage'. We know it as the motor car. Most cars are powered by a petrol engine, which burns petrol as fuel.

The picture above shows one kind of truck, or lorry. Trucks are heavy motor vehicles that carry all kinds of loads. They have a different kind of engine, called a diesel engine.

You can see the fastest motor vehicle on the race tracks. The racing car above is built purely for speed. It has a very powerful engine and can do over 250 kilometres per hour.

The car below is quite different. It has a small engine and is slow. But it can carry four people, and it does not use much fuel.

Cars are changing all the time. Car makers change the shape so that the car will slip more easily through the air. This saves fuel. Car makers also try to make their vehicles as safe as possible. They make the part surrounding the passengers very strong so that it does not collapse if the car crashes. They test their designs very carefully. In the picture below they are crashing their cars on purpose, to see just what happens.

# Inside the car

There are thousands of different parts in a car. It is the most complicated machine we use every day. We can think of the various parts of a car as working together in groups, or systems. Different systems have been given different colours in this picture of an ordinary family car. In this car the driver sits on the left. This is called 'left-hand drive'.

In this car the engine is at the front, and it drives the back wheels. This is called rear-wheel drive. Other cars have front-wheel drive. The engine drives the front wheels. In a few cars the engine is at the back. This car has a closed-in body. It is called a saloon. Cars called convertibles have an open top, which you can cover up with a hood. Estate cars have a long body with plenty of room at the back to carry luggage. The rear seats can be folded down to give even more room.

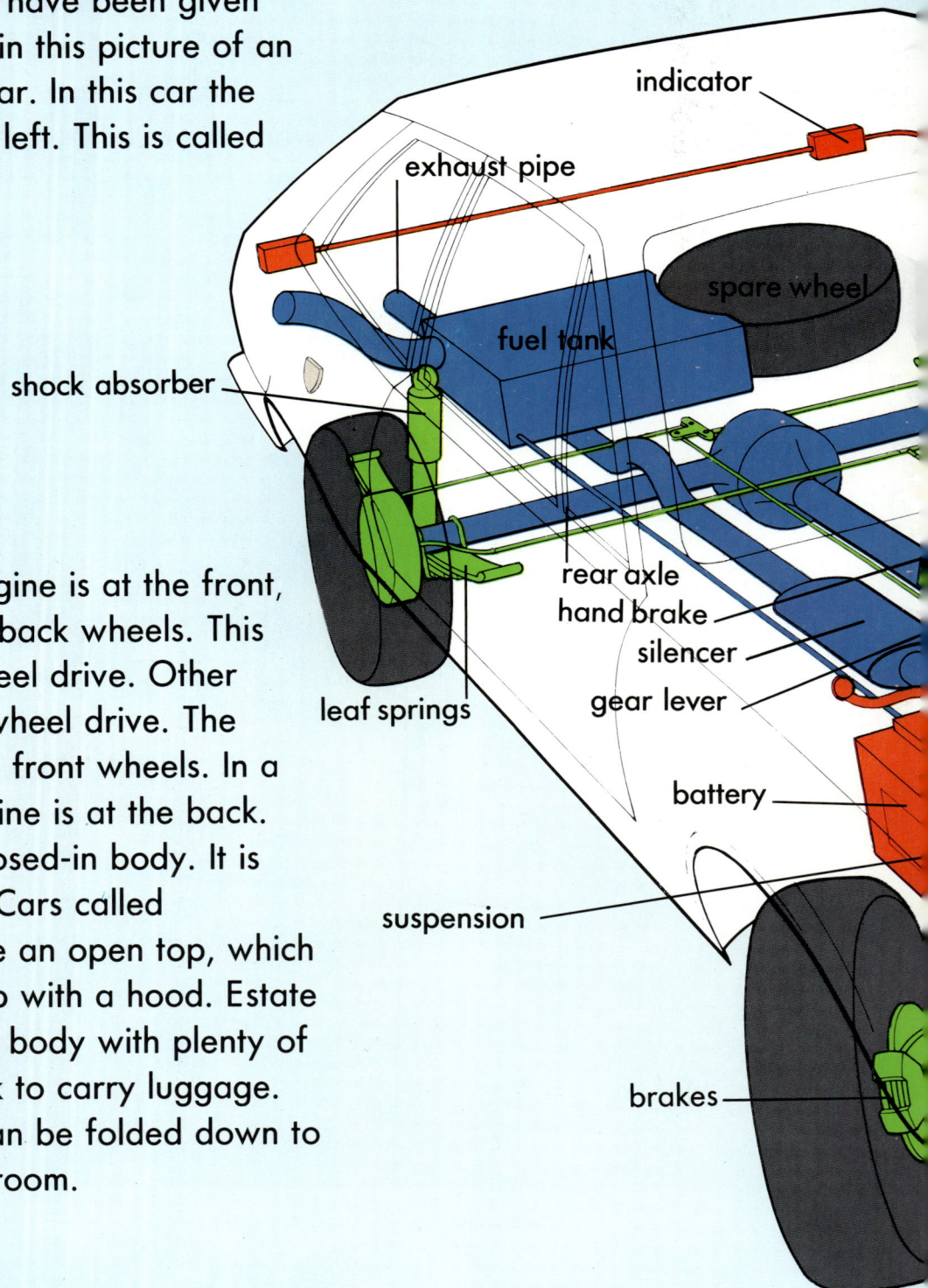

indicator

exhaust pipe

spare wheel

fuel tank

shock absorber

rear axle

hand brake

silencer

gear lever

leaf springs

battery

suspension

brakes

The engine and the transmission system are coloured blue. The transmission carries power from the engine to the driving wheels. Parts of the braking and steering systems are coloured green. The suspension system is also coloured green. The parts of the electrical system are coloured red. You can learn more about these systems on pages 50 and 51.

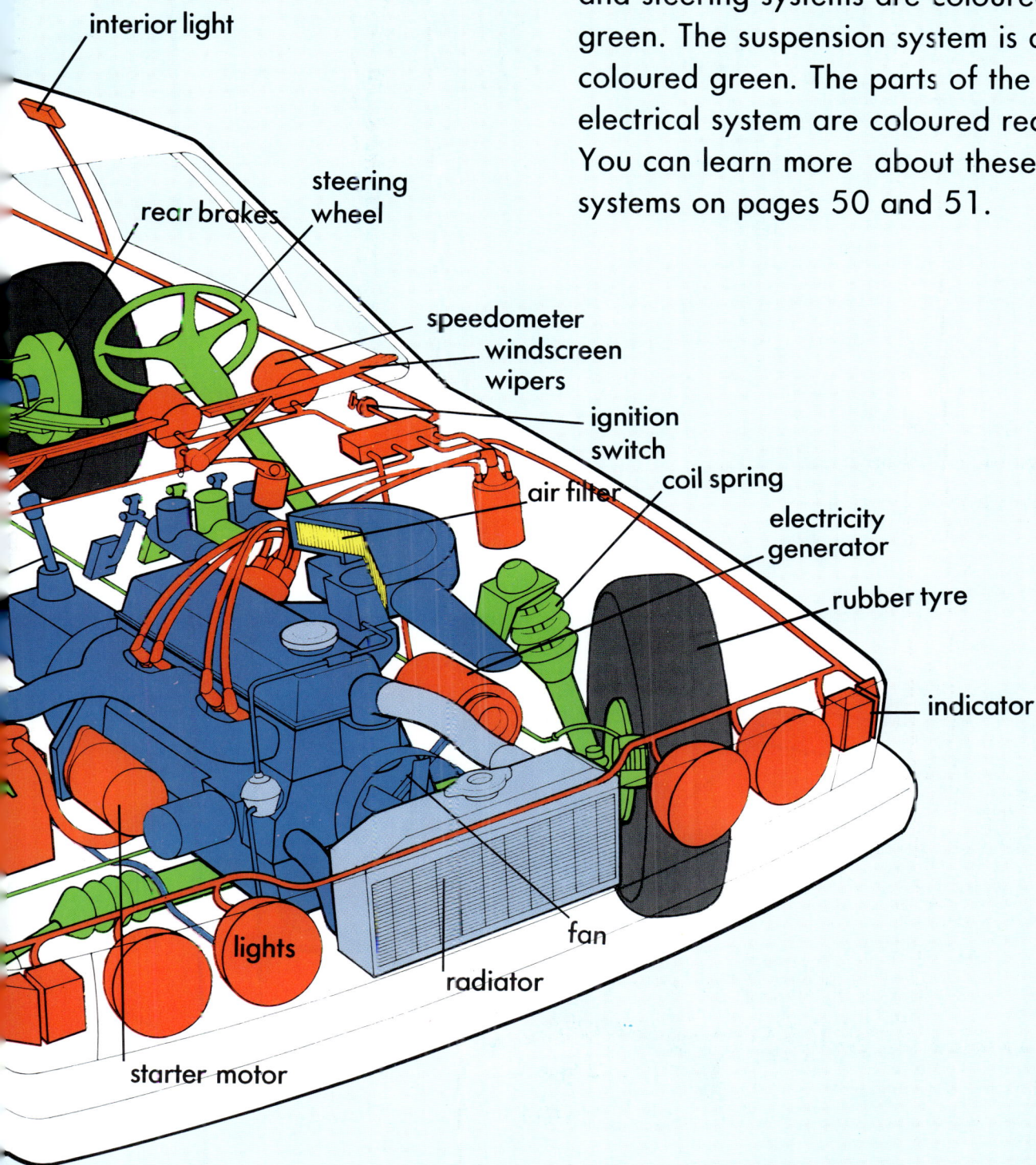

interior light

steering wheel

rear brakes

speedometer

windscreen wipers

ignition switch

air filter

coil spring

electricity generator

rubber tyre

indicator

lights

fan

radiator

starter motor

## Parts of the car

The engine burns petrol, which is stored in the fuel tank. Gears in the gearbox help the engine drive the car at different speeds. The propeller shaft carries the power to the rear axle. This turns the driving wheels.

Every car has two kinds of brakes. The main foot brakes are worked by a pedal. They work on all four wheels. The hand brake works on the rear wheels.

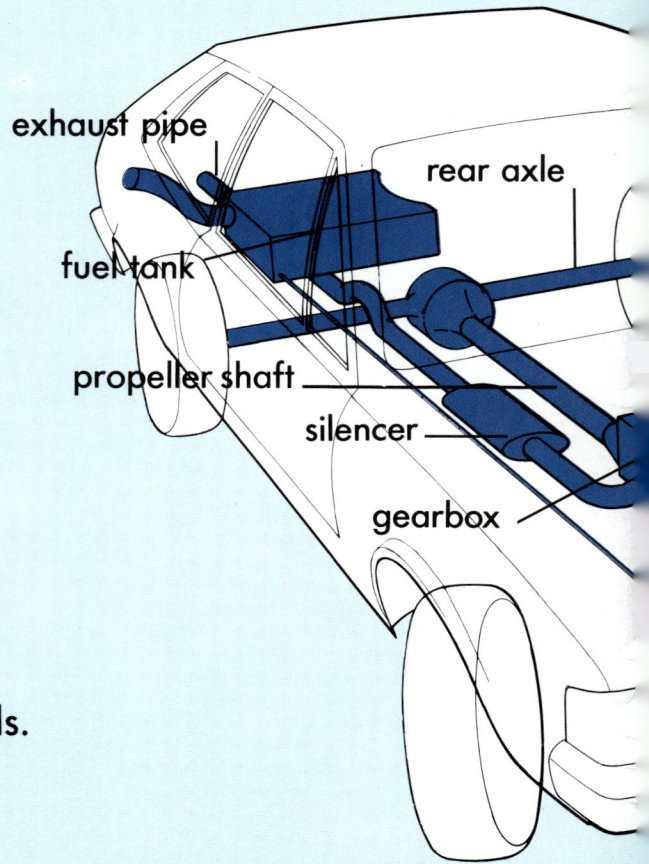

exhaust pipe

rear axle

fuel tank

propeller shaft

silencer

gearbox

braking, steering and suspension system

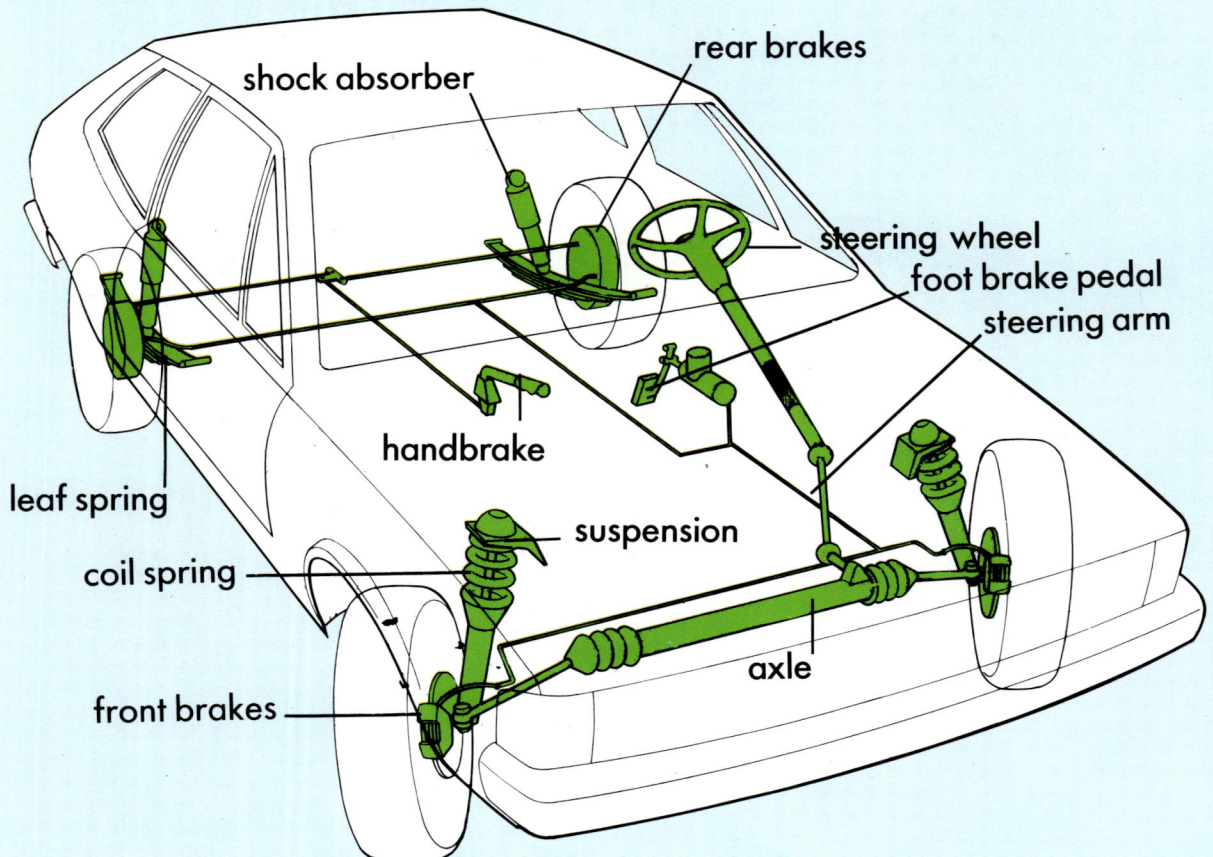

shock absorber

rear brakes

steering wheel
foot brake pedal
steering arm

handbrake

suspension

leaf spring

coil spring

axle

front brakes

**engine and transmission system**

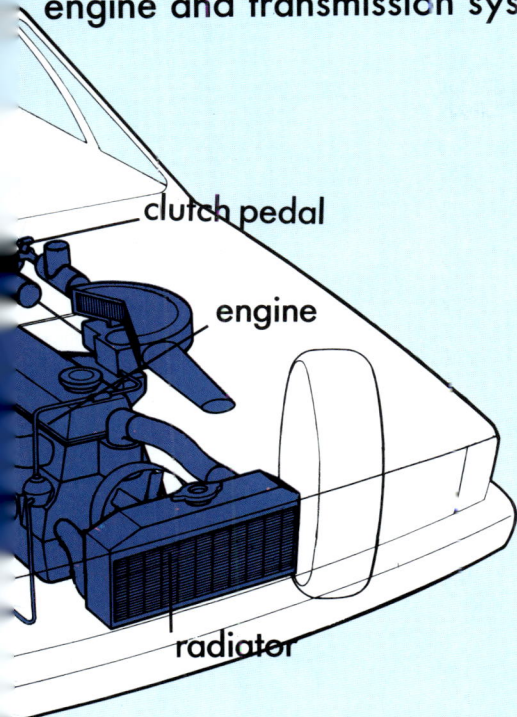

clutch pedal

engine

radiator

The springs and shock absorbers of the suspension system help give the passengers a comfortable ride. The steering system allows the driver to steer the car in the right direction.

The electrical system is used to make sparks to burn the fuel in the engine. The electricity comes from a battery. Electricity is put back into the battery by a generator. Electricity is also used to run the lights, the windscreen wipers and other instruments.

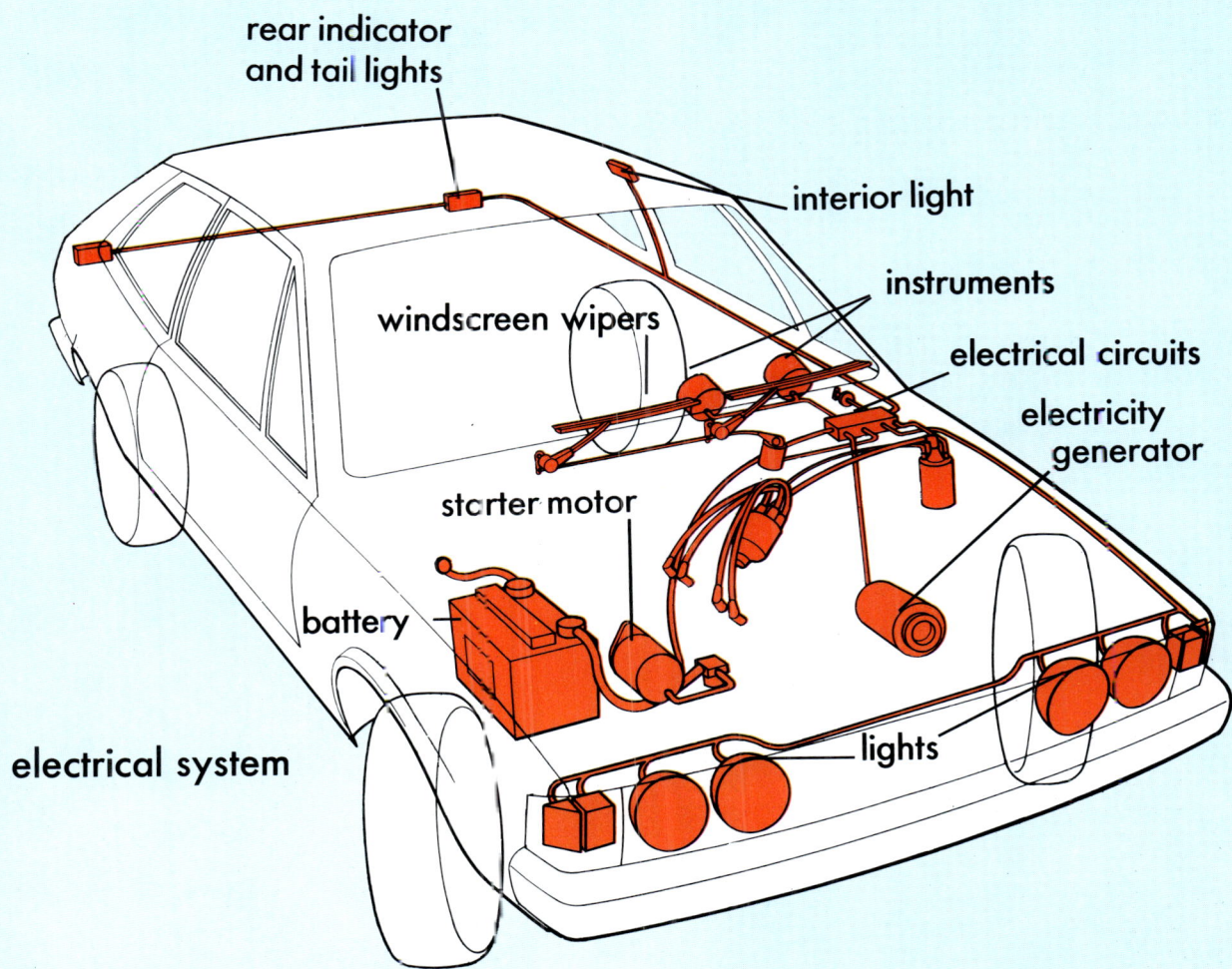

rear indicator and tail lights

interior light

instruments

electrical circuits

electricity generator

windscreen wipers

starter motor

battery

electrical system

lights

# POWERING MACHINES

## Animal power

Years ago there were no engines to drive machines. Muscle power was used instead. Many people kept strong animals like horses or oxen. They used these animals to do the heavy work. In many parts of the world, animals are still used, mainly for pulling carts and wagons.

Ponies are used in some coal mines for hauling coal wagons.

Eskimoes use dog sledges to travel aross the frozen snow. The dogs they use are huskies. These are powerful, hardworking dogs.

In some countries oxen are used to power old water pumps. The ox moves round. This turns gears. The big wheel with buckets moves round.

# Power from wind and sun

The power of the wind has been used to drive machines for hundreds of years. Windmills were used to grind grain into flour. Today windmills are used in some countries to pump water. Three of these machines are shown in the picture below. The wind turns the sails, and the sails drive the pumps.

We are now beginning to use another kind of natural power – the power of the sun. We call this solar power.

The calculator above works by solar power. Tiny cells change sunlight into electricity.

## Water power

There is a lot of power in water when it is flowing fast. Waterwheels driven by rivers were used for hundreds of years. They turned grindstones and drove machinery. The picture shows a pair of waterwheels that are still working.

We use a different kind of waterwheel today to make electricity. We call it a water turbine.

Dams are built across rivers. The force of the water drives the turbines. This is called hydro-electric power.

# Steam power

Water turns into steam when it boils. The steam is full of power. We can use this power to drive engines. Inside the steam engine, the steam pushes a piston down a cylinder. The movement of the piston turns wheels or drives other machinery. The picture on the right shows an old fire-pump driven by steam. Water is boiled into steam, which pumps out water through a hosepipe.

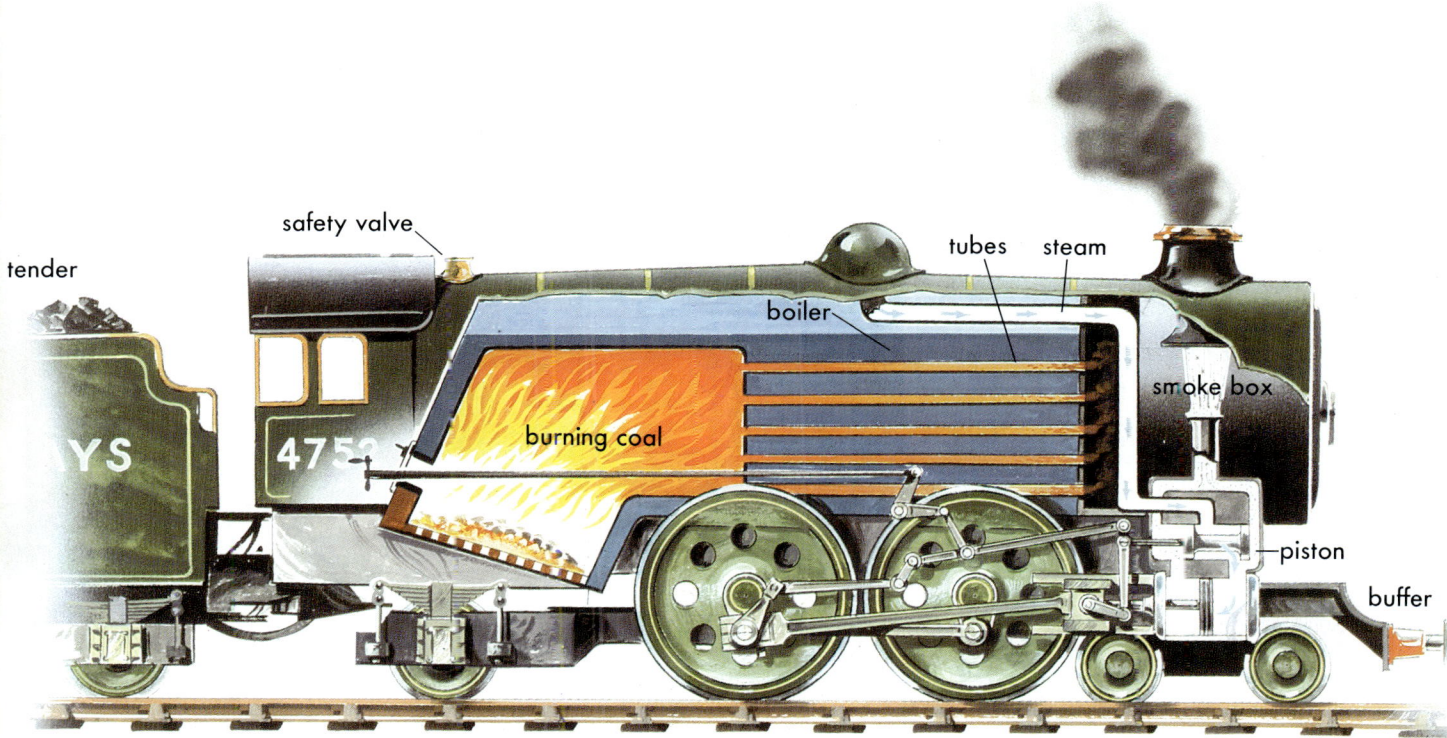

safety valve

tender

tubes   steam

boiler

smoke box

burning coal

YS   4752

piston

buffer

In a steam locomotive the coal fire makes flames and hot gases. These heat the water in the boiler.

The water turns into steam, which pushes against the piston. As the piston moves, it turns the wheels.

## Power stations

The electricity we use in our homes is made in power stations. They use engines called turbines, which are driven by steam. Inside a turbine there are kinds of spinning wheels. They turn round when steam passes through them. The spinning turbine turns machines called generators, which make the electricity. The picture below shows the turbine hall at a power station.

nuclear reactor

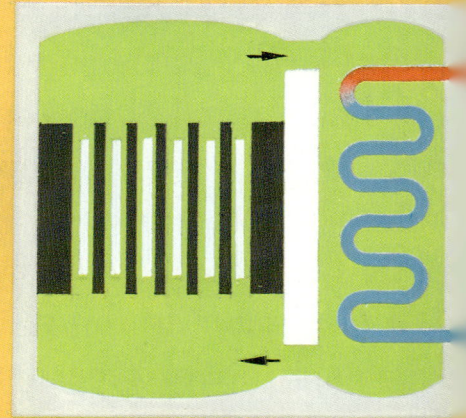

power
grid

turbine

water
supply

In some power stations the steam is made in nuclear boilers. These use the heat given out in a nuclear reactor like the one on the left. A reactor contains a metal called uranium, which gives out heat when it breaks down.

The power station below burns coal to make steam. The tall towers are used for cooling water from the turbines.

# Petrol and diesel power

This is a picture of a car engine. The diagrams on the right show what happens inside the cylinder. As the piston goes down, fuel goes in. As the piston goes up, it squeezes the mixture. This explodes, forcing the piston down again. Burnt gases are pushed out by the piston.

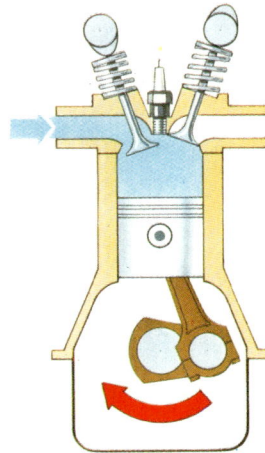

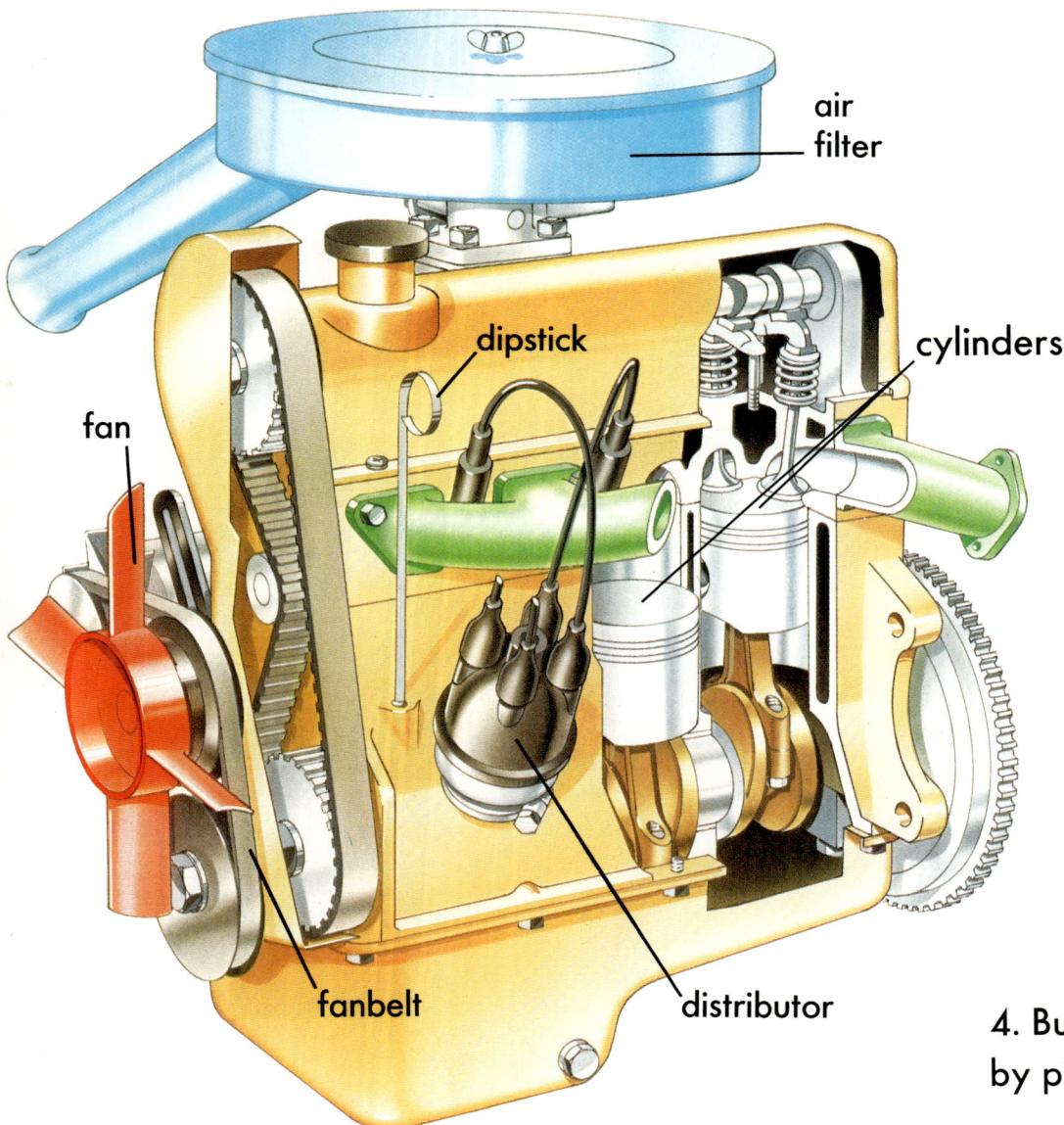

1. Piston goes down, fuel goes in

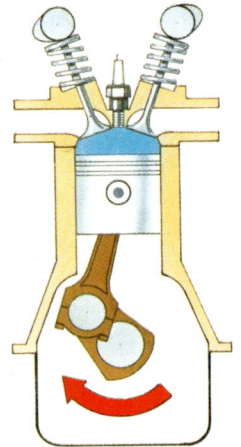

2. Piston goes up. It squeezes the mixtur‹

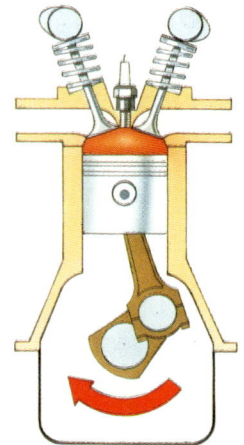

3. Mixture explodes. Piston is forced down

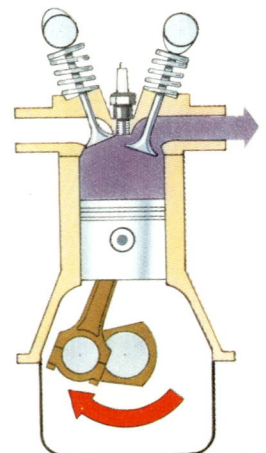

4. Burnt gases are pushed ‹ by piston

air filter

dipstick

cylinders

fan

fanbelt

distributor

This engine is inside a giant ship. It is a diesel engine. The inventor was Rudolf Diesel. Oil is burned instead of petrol. The oil burns when it meets hot air inside the cylinders. This makes power to turn the engines.

## Jets and rockets

Most aircraft have a kind of engine called a jet engine. Air is taken in and heated by burning fuel. The hot air is pushed through a jet or a turbine, an engine which works a bit like a simple pinwheel. The air shoots out of the rear of the engine at very high speed. This moves the aircraft forwards.

pinwheel

jet engine

60

Rockets work rather like jet engines. They are pushed forwards when a stream of gases shoots backwards. This is what happens when you let go of a blown-up ballon. Jet engines need air to work, but rockets can work in space, where there is no air. Simple rockets have many uses. They can carry a line to a shipwreck.

# Electric motors

An electric motor works by a magnet inside it. A coil of wire is inside too. Electricity passes along this wire. This makes the wire magnetic. When the wire meets the magnet two things happen. It tries to push closer to the magnet and then to pull away from it. This pushing and pulling works the motor.

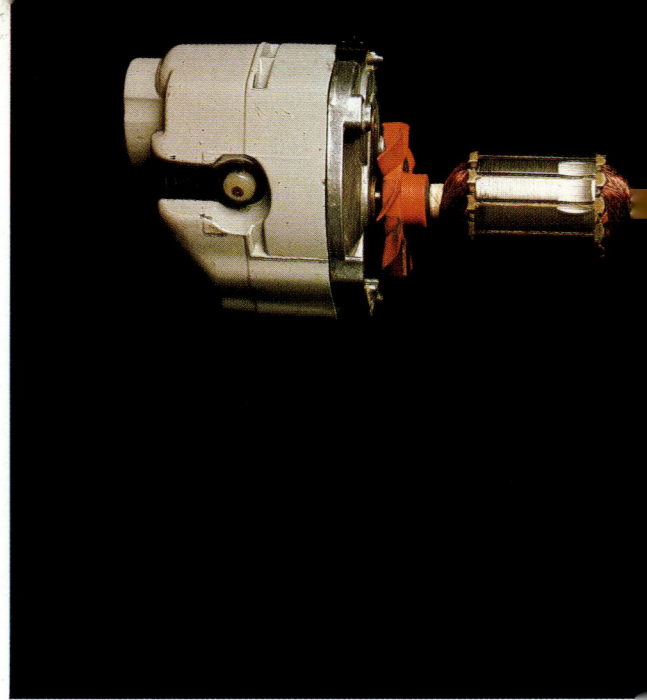

electric motor

One end of a magnet is called the north. The other is called the south. They try to pull together.

The two north ends push each other apart. So do the south ends.

The picture below shows a simple electric motor. The block can spin round between the ends of a magnet. The electricity from the battery passes into the coils of wire. This turns the block into a magnet. The pushing and pulling between the two magnets make the rod spin round The spinning rod turns the gears and makes the wheels move.

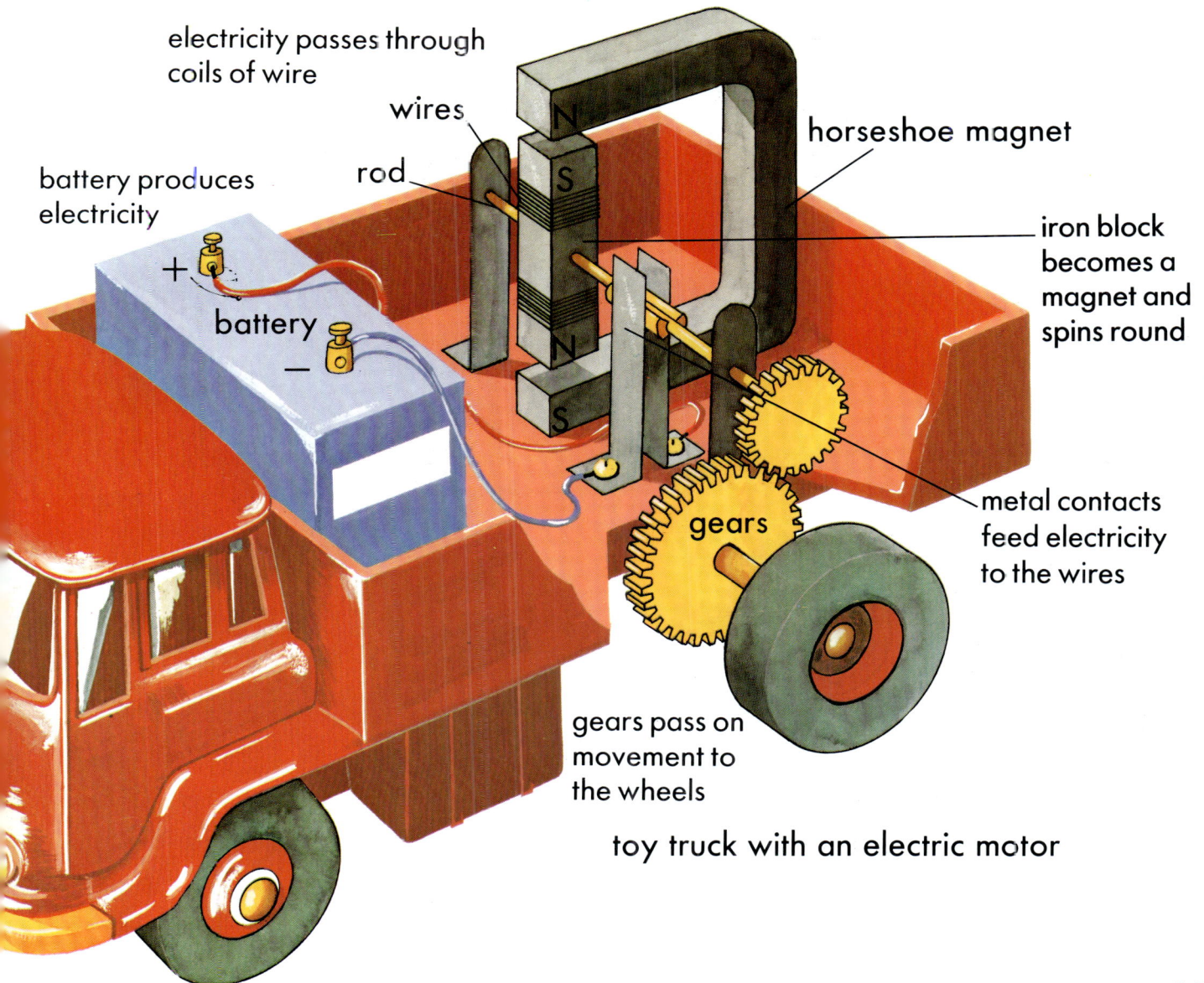

electricity passes through coils of wire

wires

rod

battery produces electricity

+

battery

−

N

S

N

S

horseshoe magnet

iron block becomes a magnet and spins round

metal contacts feed electricity to the wires

gears

gears pass on movement to the wheels

toy truck with an electric motor

# DID YOU KNOW?

The biggest cuckoo clock in the world is eight metres high. It has a very large cuckoo inside it!

A big popcorn factory produced 65 million packets of popcorn in a single year.

This lady is cleaning the world's longest staircase, in Norway. There are 3,875 steps in the building.

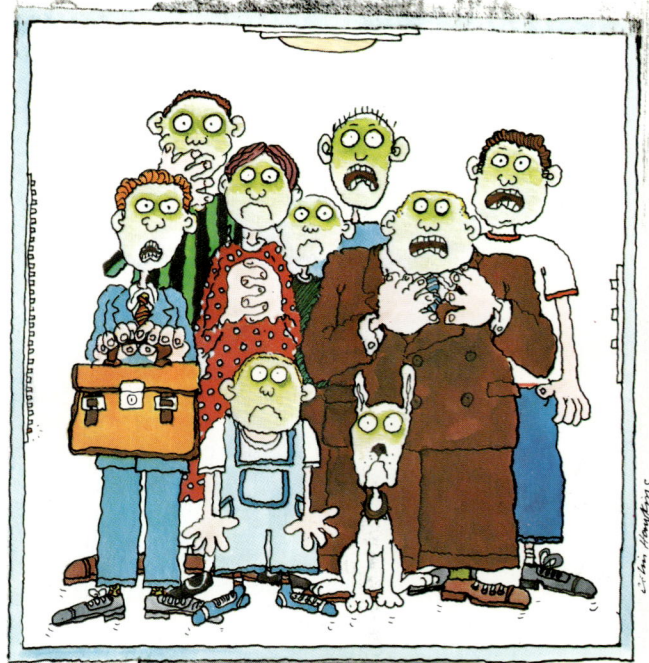

The world's fastest lift moves 600 metres per minute. Do you think these people are enjoying the ride?

# INDEX